HISTORY OF HOLIDAYS AND FESTIVALS

RAMADAN AND EID AL-FITR

BY BEV CRAWFORD

CONTENT CONSULTANT
Dr. Sana Tayyen
Assistant Professor of Religious Studies
University of Redlands

Cover image: On Eid al-Fitr, many Muslims gather at mosques to perform prayers. Some visit the mosque at the Taj Mahal in Agra, India.

Core Library
An Imprint of Abdo Publishing
abdobooks.com

abdobooks.com

Published by Abdo Publishing, a division of ABDO, PO Box 398166, Minneapolis, Minnesota 55439.

Printed in the United States of America, North Mankato, Minnesota.
102023
012024

THIS BOOK CONTAINS RECYCLED MATERIALS

Cover Photo: Pawan Sharma/AFP/Getty Images
Interior Photos: Ali Jadallah/Anadolu Agency/Getty Images, 4–5; Debarchan Chatterjee/NurPhoto/Getty Images, 8; Shakil Adil/AP Images, 11, 45; Mamunur Rashid/NurPhoto/AP Images, 12–13, 43; Shutterstock Images, 14 (doors), 14 (icons); Ali Najafi/AFP/Getty Images, 17; Abdel Ghani Bashir/AFP/Getty Images, 18; Arif Hudaverdi Yaman/Anadolu Agency/Getty Images, 20; Beinecke Rare Book & Manuscript Library/Yale University, 22–23; Smith Collection/Gado Images/Alamy, 26; Red Line Editorial, 28; Anjum Naveed/AP Images, 30–31; Rasool Ali/Moment/Getty Images, 32; Fatemeh Bahrami/Anadolu Agency/Getty Images, 34; Khalid Tanveer/AP Images, 39; Avishek Das/SOPA Images/LightRocket/Getty Images, 40

Editor: Laura Stickney
Series Designer: Ryan Gale

Library of Congress Control Number: 2023940254

Publisher's Cataloging-in-Publication Data
Names: Crawford, Bev, author.
Title: Ramadan and Eid al-Fitr / by Bev Crawford
Description: Minneapolis, Minnesota: Abdo Publishing, 2024 | Series: History of holidays and festivals | Includes online resources and index.
Identifiers: ISBN 9781098292638 (lib. bdg.) | ISBN 9798384910572 (ebook)
Subjects: LCSH: Holidays--Juvenile literature. | Fasts and feasts--Juvenile literature. | Ramadan--Juvenile literature. | Īd al-Fiṭr--Juvenile literature. | Festival of Breaking Fast (Islam)--Juvenile literature. | Islam--Rituals--Juvenile literature.
Classification: DDC 297.362--dc23

CONTENTS

CHAPTER ONE

A FAMILY RAMADAN

Amir wakes up early, before the sun rises. It is time to begin the *sawm*, or fast, for the holy month of Ramadan. Amir and his family are Muslims, or followers of the religion of Islam. Ramadan is the most important month in Islam. It is a time to focus on Allah, or God. During Ramadan, Muslims do not eat or drink anything during daylight hours. This is the second year Amir is fasting for Ramadan. Every day for a month, Amir and his family wake up before sunrise to eat a special

In some places, *musaharati* wake people up for suhoor. They walk through the streets banging drums, singing, and reciting poems. Sometimes they wear traditional clothing.

meal called *suhoor.* This prepares them for the day of fasting. A healthy suhoor helps provide enough energy to get through the day without eating or drinking. Amir likes to eat eggs, cheese, bread, and fruit. One morning every Ramadan, his family makes a special trip to a pancake restaurant for a suhoor treat.

Amir's little sister, Kinza, is too young to fast. So during Ramadan, she focuses on doing good deeds. The family's mosque is having a toy drive, so Kinza plans to donate some of her toys. Last year, Kinza made a colorful paper lantern, a traditional symbol of Ramadan.

On most days during Ramadan, Amir's family cooks together to prepare *iftar*. This is the evening meal that breaks each day's fast. It takes place after sunset. Traditionally, Muslims end their fast with a sip of water and dates, a sweet fruit native to the Middle East. Then they have iftar. During iftar, families and neighbors visit each other to share foods made especially for Ramadan.

Both Amir and Kinza have a special iftar treat box, which has 30 compartments for counting the 30 days of Ramadan. Each evening before iftar, they open a door on their treat boxes to reveal a piece of candy. Every night after the meal, they have special Ramadan desserts. Their favorite is *qatayef*, pancakes soaked in sugar syrup and stuffed with cheese, walnuts, or cream.

SUHOOR AND IFTAR FOODS

Muslims must eat a healthy suhoor to prepare for the day's fast. This may include protein-rich foods such as eggs, yogurt, beans, fish, and chicken. Whole grains such as bread and oatmeal provide vitamins and energy. People may also eat nuts and fruit. For iftar, Muslims traditionally begin by having water and dates. They also eat healthy dinner foods such as lentil and vegetable soups, chicken, fish, and beans.

Amir and Kinza most look forward to Eid al-Fitr, the Festival of Breaking the Fast. This happens at the end of Ramadan. On Eid al-Fitr, Amir and Kinza will receive new clothes and gifts. They will go to the mosque and join in prayers. There will be lots of food for everyone to enjoy. And no fasting will be allowed.

On Eid al-Fitr, many Muslims take part in special morning prayers at mosques. Some places hold outdoor community prayer services for large groups of people.

THE HOLY MONTH

The religion of Islam began more than 1,400 years ago in the Middle East. Islam was founded by the prophet Muhammad. He was an important Arab religious leader who was born in the city of Mecca, located in what is now Saudi Arabia, around 570 CE. Muslims believe Muhammad was a prophet who received revelations from Allah. These revelations were collected and made into the Qur'an, the holy book of Islam.

During Ramadan, Muslims fast to grow closer to Allah. During the 30-day fast, all healthy adult Muslims must avoid food and drink during daylight hours. This includes water. Smoking, cursing, fighting, and gossiping are not allowed, either. Children can begin fasting around ages seven to ten. By not satisfying their hunger, Muslims are encouraged to think about Allah and self-improvement. Fasting helps teach patience, compassion, and gratitude. It is also an experience shared with fellow Muslims, helping people build community. When Muslims fast, they feel more understanding toward those who are less fortunate.

In Islam, some people are excused from the Ramadan fast. This includes young children, ill or elderly people, and pregnant women. It also includes people who are traveling and people who need to take medicine with food. If people miss fasting because they are sick or traveling, they must make up the missed

> ## PERSPECTIVES
> ### FASTING DURING RAMADAN
> **Fasting during Ramadan can be challenging for kids. But it can help teach them important lessons. Ali, a 14-year-old Muslim boy, explains that fasting is "just to feel how the poor people feel. They don't get to have a lot of water and food." Ali says fasting during school can be hard. He and his cousins fast at school while their non-Muslim classmates eat lunch. "Sometimes we have football games, and we still play, but we don't drink water," he says. Ali started fasting for Ramadan when he was ten years old. "It was really hard back then, but you get more used to it," he says.**

days when they are better. People who are unable to fast must focus on doing good deeds instead.

More than 1,000 years ago, Muhammad and his followers observed the first Ramadan. They fasted and recited verses from the Qur'an. Today, Muslims around the world celebrate Ramadan in the same ways. They fast, read the Qur'an, perform good deeds, and join in community meals. They perform special

During Ramadan, some mosques offer free iftar meals for members of the community. Volunteers help prepare and arrange food for worshippers.

evening prayers called *Taraweeh* too. New traditions have also developed over time. Across the globe, Ramadan continues to be an important religious holiday.

EXPLORE ONLINE

Chapter One discusses how one family observes Ramadan. The video at the website below explores another person's experience of Ramadan. How is Ramadan different for the girl narrating the video? How is it the same? What new information did you learn from the video?

RAMADAN

abdocorelibrary.com/ramadan-and-eid-al-fitr

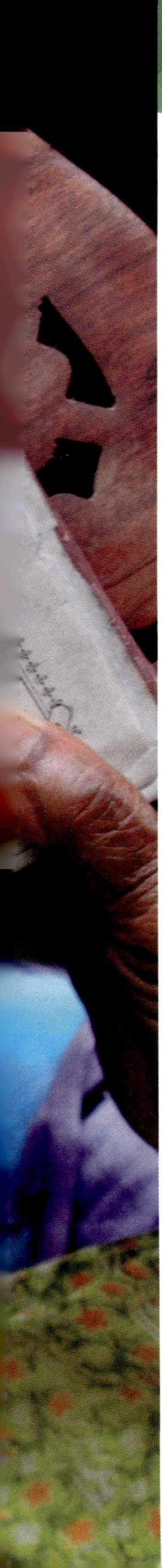

CHAPTER TWO

THE ORIGINS OF RAMADAN

Muslims believe that during the month of Ramadan in 610 CE, the prophet Muhammad saw the angel Jibreel, or Gabriel. When Jibreel spoke, Muhammad became a prophet. He began receiving revelations from Allah. The night of this first revelation is called Laylat al-Qadr, or Night of Power. The exact night on which this occurred is unknown. But some people believe that it was one of the final ten nights of Ramadan.

The Qur'an is divided into 114 sections called sūrahs. These are further divided into a total of more than 6,000 verses.

THE FIVE PILLARS OF ISLAM

Shahadah
Declaration of faith

Salat
Five daily prayers

Zakat
Acts of charity and kindness

Sawm
Fasting

Hajj
Pilgrimage to Mecca

The core religious practices for Muslims are often called the Five Pillars of Islam. These involve prayers, acts of charity, and fasting. Why do you think these practices are important for Muslims? What role do they play during Ramadan?

In 613 CE, Muhammad began sharing the revelations he received with people in Mecca. His family members became his first followers. But other people in the city were angry about Muhammad's teachings. They persecuted Muhammad and his followers, who became known as Muslims. In 622 CE, the Muslims fled

Mecca and traveled to Medina, another city in Saudi Arabia. People in Medina were more accepting. Many became Muslims.

In 624 CE, Muhammad received a revelation from Allah that commanded Muslims to fast for 30 days. According to the Qur'an, the revelation said Muslims must fast for one month. It also gave instructions about making up missed days and what to do if a person cannot fast. Fasting during Ramadan became a unique part of the early Muslim community. Christians and Jews lived in Medina too. These religious groups also fasted. But Muslims were the only group that routinely fasted for so many days. Fasting during Ramadan helped Muslims create their own religious identity.

For Muslims in the 600s, a suhoor meal might have included only a few dates and some water. Iftar consisted of whatever people could find, such as roasted flour mixed with crushed dates or olive oil. Muhammad urged his followers to share meals with other Muslims who had no food. This developed into

PERSPECTIVES

THE MEANING OF IFTAR

For many Muslims, iftar is a time to gather, connect, and share with family and friends. Shafi Musaddique, a journalist from London, United Kingdom, remembers enjoying family iftar meals as a teen. "Seeing the smiles on everyone's faces, and the shared satisfaction taken from breaking the fast together, was really joyous," Musaddique said. Sarah, a marketing manager from Egypt, shares a similar view of iftar meals. "The best iftars are the ones with family gatherings and my grandma cooking all the food I love. There is an incredible sense of unity," she says.

the tradition of inviting friends, family, and people in need to share iftar together.

Muslims observe Laylat al-Qadr as a part of Ramadan too. On this night, they believe that angels descend to Earth for a night of peace, blessings, and guidance from Allah. Muslims observe the night with solemn prayers, which can sometimes last all night. Some Muslims donate money or do good deeds on Laylat al-Qadr. The rewards of giving are believed to be especially generous on this night.

On Laylat al-Qadr, some Muslims place copies of the Qur'an on top of their heads while reciting prayers. This is seen as an act of respect and honor toward Allah.

THE SPREAD OF ISLAM

Muhammad and his followers created a new religious community. Many people joined their movement. In 630 CE, Muslims returned to Mecca. After Muhammad died in 632 CE, his successors maintained leadership in Islam. Through Arab expansion and trade, Islam spread far beyond the Middle East. Muslims resettled

During Ramadan, millions of Muslims travel to the Grand Mosque in Mecca. They pray around a large, cube-shaped structure called the Kaaba.

in other areas too. They brought their religion to southern Europe, North Africa, and central and South Asia. Eventually, Muslims gained leadership over many regions of the world. They built several empires, such as the Ottoman Empire (1300s–1922) in the region around Turkey and the Mughal Empire (1526–1857) in India.

Islamic leaders wanted to collect all of Muhammad's revelations into one written text. Some Muslims had memorized all the revelations. These people were called *qurra*, or reciters. They taught the revelations to others. All written copies of these texts were collected and compared to the qurra's recitations. Each written part was confirmed by recitations from at least two qurra. Around 650 CE, the first written copy of the Qur'an was complete.

PRACTICING ISLAM

Like Christianity and Judaism, Islam is a monotheistic religion. This means Muslims believe there is only one God. The beliefs and practices of Islam are based on the revelations of Muhammad. One practice involves daily prayer to Allah. Muslims pray five times a day, at dawn, noon, midafternoon, sunset, and in the evening. They pray facing the direction of Mecca, which is considered the holiest city in Islam. Another practice involves making a pilgrimage to Mecca. Muslims who can afford it are expected to visit Mecca at least once in their lifetime to perform rituals at holy sites.

LOCAL CUSTOMS

As Islam spread, many people converted to the religion. People often kept their own local customs when they became Muslims. In the 600s CE, a *musaharati*, or awakener, walked the streets of Cairo, Egypt, before dawn. He sounded the wake-up call for suhoor. Today, many Muslims use alarm

The iftar cannon is still used in countries such as Turkey and the United Arab Emirates. On each day of Ramadan, the cannon is fired to mark the end of fasting for the day.

clocks or smartphones to wake up. But a musaharati still makes the rounds in many places. In Morocco, he plays a trumpet. In Gaza, he plays a drum. In Yemen, the neighborhood musaharati knocks on people's doors. In the Republic of Sudan, a group of 20 to 30 men walk through the streets drumming, singing, and chanting.

Another Ramadan custom began in the 1500s in Cairo, Egypt. A wealthy sultan marked iftar by firing a cannon at sunset. The iftar cannon is still fired today in some Middle Eastern and North African countries.

STRAIGHT TO THE SOURCE

Muslims follow the revelations Muhammad received from Allah, which are collected in the Qur'an. Sūrah 2 verse 185 of the Qur'an discusses what Muslims should do during Ramadan:

> *It was in the month of Ramadan that the Qur'an was revealed as a guidance for mankind, clear messages giving guidance and distinguishing between right and wrong. So any one of you who [is present] in that month should fast, and anyone who is ill or on a journey should make up for the lost days by fasting on other days later. God wants ease for you, not hardship. He wants you to complete the prescribed period and to glorify Him for having guided you, so that you may be thankful.*

Source: *The Qur'an.* Translation by M. A. S. Abdel Haleem. Oxford UP, 2004, p. 20.

CONSIDER YOUR AUDIENCE

Adapt this passage for a different audience, such as your principal or friends. Write a blog post conveying this same information for the new audience. How does your post differ from the original text and why?

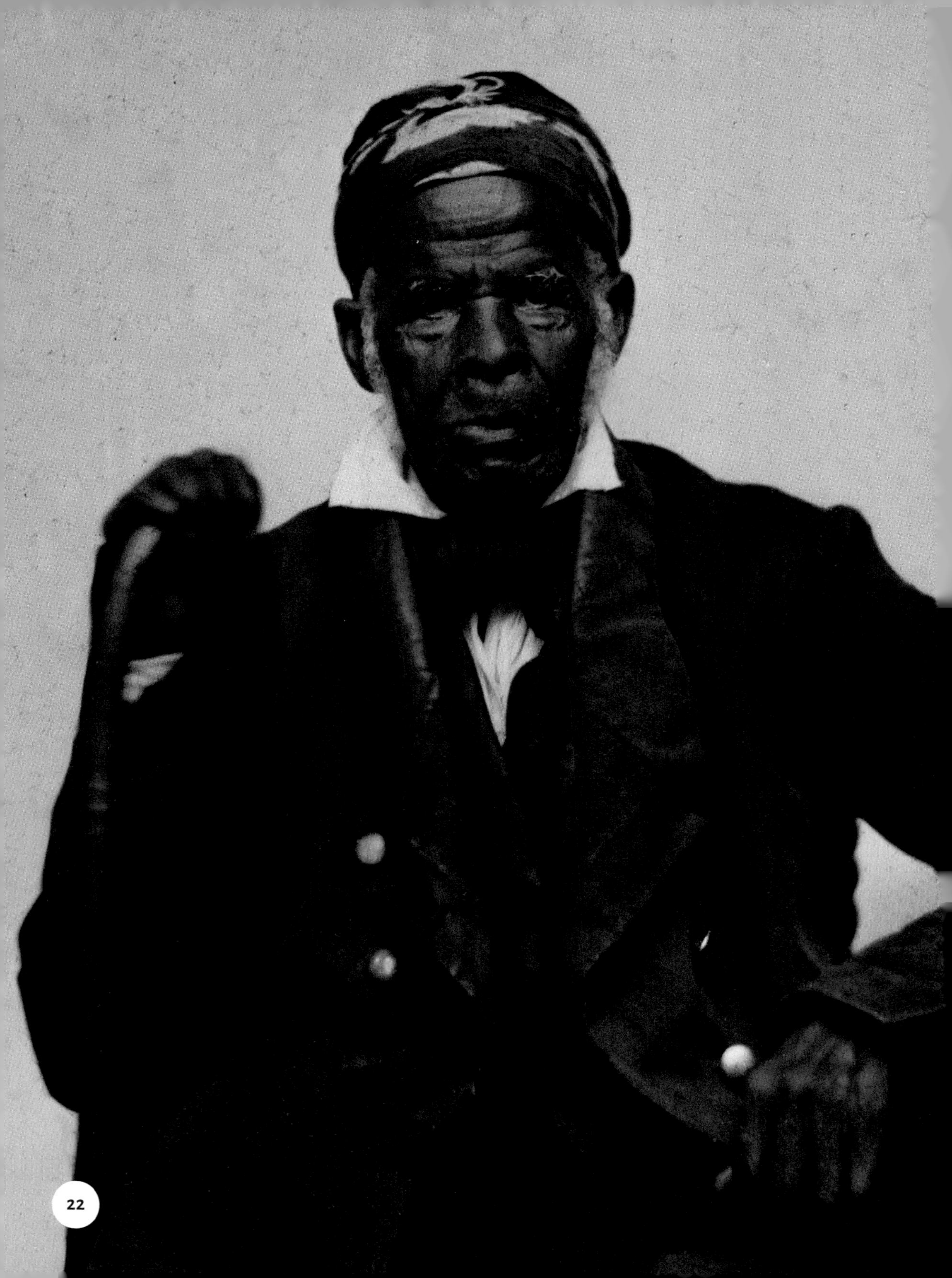

CHAPTER THREE

ISLAM IN THE UNITED STATES

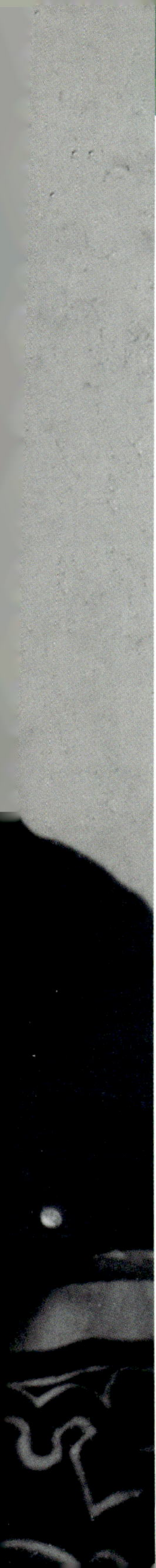

Over time, Islam spread to many countries. It traveled to what is now the United States through the slave trade. As early as the 1500s, Europeans began capturing and enslaving people from regions of Africa. The Spanish brought enslaved people from West Africa to the Caribbean islands, where they were forced to do difficult work for no pay. In the 1600s and 1700s, the Dutch, English, and French joined the slave trade. By this time, the Caribbean and other parts of

Omar ibn Said was an enslaved Muslim man in the United States. His writings have helped historians learn about West African culture, religion, and education in the 1800s.

OMAR IBN SAID

Omar ibn Said was born around 1770 in what is now Senegal, a country in West Africa. He was a Muslim scholar who studied Islam and Arabic. Said was captured, enslaved, and put on a ship to South Carolina. Unlike most other enslaved Muslims, Said's enslaver allowed him to continue practicing Islam. Said prayed five times a day and observed Ramadan. He wrote prayers in Arabic and tacked them to trees. In 1831, Said wrote his autobiography, *The Life of Omar Ibn Said*, in Arabic. The book was later translated into English.

North America were controlled by several European countries. By the late 1800s, between 10 and 12 million Africans had been enslaved and transported to the Americas.

Islam had spread from the Middle East to nations in Africa. Historians estimate that one-third of all enslaved people in the Americas came from Muslim parts of West Africa. Many of these enslaved people were forced to convert to Christianity. But some secretly continued practicing Islam.

Some enslaved African Muslims had attended universities in Africa. They had memorized the entire Qur'an. Some enslaved African Muslims used their education to write letters and diaries in Arabic. They also communicated with other enslaved African Muslims in Arabic. White enslavers sometimes took advantage of educated enslaved Muslims by making them work as bookkeepers, personal servants, and coachmen. Some enslaved Muslims traveled with their enslavers and learned about Western business practices. Some were allowed to practice Islam openly by praying, fasting during Ramadan, and wearing religious clothing. But many other enslaved Muslims were forbidden from following their religious practices.

MUSLIM BLACK AMERICANS AND IMMIGRANTS

In the 1860s, Northern and Southern states fought over the issue of slavery in the American Civil War (1861–1865). In 1865, the war ended and slavery was

Throughout the late 1800s and early 1900s, Muslims immigrated to the United States in large numbers. Many came from countries such as Lebanon, Syria, and Jordan.

abolished, or outlawed, in the United States. Many Black Muslims were no longer enslaved. Because Christianity was seen as the white enslavers' religion, some Black Americans turned to Islam during this time.

In the late 1800s, more Muslim immigrants came to the United States from the Middle East and South Asia. Black Americans formed new religious communities and observed Ramadan with prayer and fasting. The first official US mosque was built in New York City in 1915.

Some Black Americans established religious groups based on Islamic practices. One was the Nation of Islam, which was founded in 1930. This group promoted Black pride and financial independence. Its members followed some practices of Islam, including observing Ramadan. But many of the group's practices went against core Islamic beliefs. For example, the group's members believed its founder, Wallace D. Fard, was Allah in human form. But a core belief of Islam is that Allah has never taken human form. Many Muslims believed the group's religion was separate

PERSPECTIVES

RAMADAN IN SPACE

During Ramadan, Muslims must do their jobs while observing the holiday. Astronaut Sultan Al Saud, for example, observed Ramadan while working in space. On June 17, 1985, he boarded a space shuttle on Ramadan. He wrote, "We had breakfast before dawn; to me it was suhoor, because I was still fasting. . . . I finished my dawn prayers on the launch pad before jumping inside the space shuttle." After the space shuttle had lifted off and reached space, Al Saud felt exhausted. He wrote, "I have one hour left until I can break my fast; the rest of the crew . . . have decided to stay with me until I break my fast. What a beautiful feeling!"

ISLAM AROUND THE WORLD

Today, Muslims live in countries all over the world. This map shows the top ten countries with the highest populations of Muslims in 2021. What do you notice about the locations of these countries?

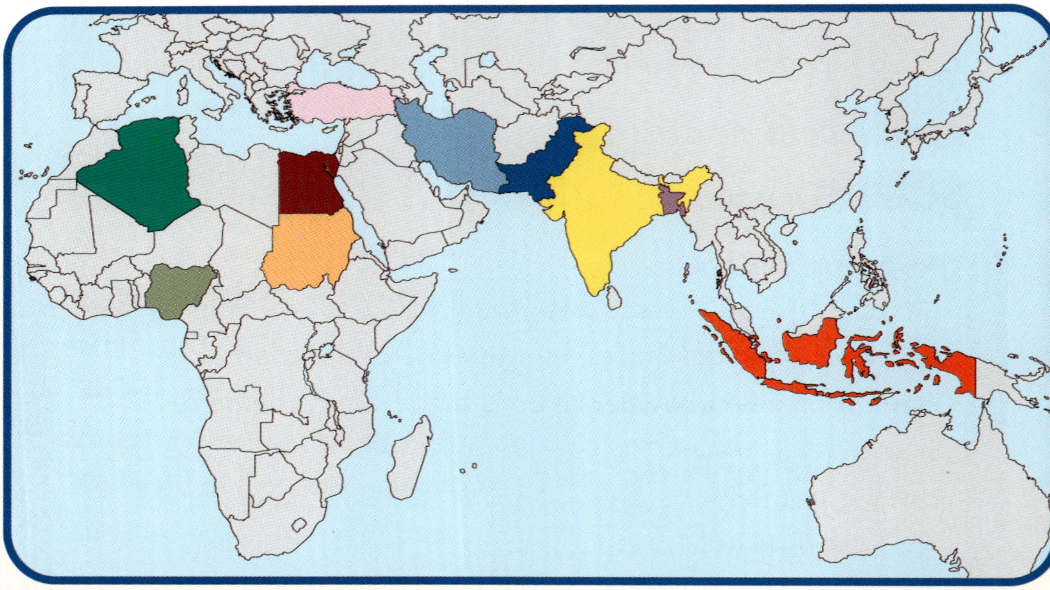

Country	Population	Country	Population
Indonesia	231,000,000	Egypt	90,000,000
Pakistan	212,300,000	Iran	82,500,000
India	200,000,000	Turkey	74,432,725
Bangladesh	153,700,000	Algeria	41,240,913
Nigeria	103,000,000	Sudan	39,585,777

from Islam. Eventually, many people left the Nation of Islam and moved toward other branches of Islam.

Over time, Muslims continued to immigrate to the United States from countries such as Egypt and Iraq. Other Muslims immigrated from South Asian countries such as Pakistan. In 2022, about 3.5 million Muslims were living in the United States.

FURTHER EVIDENCE

Chapter Three discusses what life was like for African Muslims in the early United States. Identify one of the chapter's main points. What evidence does the author provide to support this point? The website at the link below discusses this subject in more depth. Does the website support the evidence provided in the chapter? Or does it offer a new piece of evidence?

AFRICAN MUSLIMS IN EARLY AMERICA

abdocorelibrary.com/ramadan-and-eid-al-fitr

کریانہ سٹال

CHAPTER FOUR

RAMADAN TODAY

Today, Muslims all over the world observe Ramadan. Many practice the same traditions established back in Muhammad's day. Every day during Ramadan, Muslims pray together, fast, and share meals. They rise before dawn to pray and have suhoor. During daylight hours, they avoid food, drink, and smoking. Every evening, they pray and break their fast together with the iftar meal.

Many Muslims enjoy socializing after dark as they meet for communal meals. Some break

Many cities hold Ramadan bazaars or street markets, at which vendors sell traditional holiday foods such as dates.

During Ramadan, lanterns of all shapes and sizes decorate homes, shops, and streets. Some feature intricate brass designs and colorful tinted glass.

their fasts with dates, just as Muhammad did. But traditional iftar foods may differ from region to region. In Turkey, people line up at bakeries for *Ramazan pidesi*, a type of fluffy bread. In North Africa and the Middle East, people enjoy *qatayef*. In Pakistan, one popular food is *haleem*, a thick stew of meat, barley, lentils, nuts, and spices. In Ethiopia, it is traditional to eat *doro wat*, a spicy chicken stew with hard-boiled eggs. In the

United States, the Black Muslim community created bean pie, a creamy dessert made with white beans.

At night, many Muslims light colorful Ramadan *fanous*, or lanterns. These originated in ancient Egypt. Lanterns were traditionally hung at sunset for lighting and decoration during iftar. Today, people decorate their homes, businesses, and neighborhoods with colored lights and lamps. Popular colors include green, yellow, purple, and turquoise, which represent peace and spirituality. Many Ramadan lanterns and other decorations feature crescent moons and stars. While some people prefer traditional brass lanterns, modern lantern designs sometimes feature pop culture figures, cartoon characters, and athletes.

In the United States, many stores sell Ramadan and Eid al-Fitr lanterns, decorations, books, and craft kits. In Middle Eastern countries, television companies may also launch their biggest shows during this time. They often feature month-long soap operas and game shows that involve big prizes.

During Ramadan, many Muslims gather at mosques to perform *mukabalah*. This practice involves reading or reciting the Qur'an with others.

PRAYER, FASTING, AND ZAKAT

Prayer is another important part of Ramadan. Muslims may pray in public spaces by prostrating to Allah on prayer rugs. Prayer rugs give people a clean space to use for praying. During the month of Ramadan, people may go to mosques to participate in community prayer and readings with others. Muslims also recite the Taraweeh prayer in addition to their daily prayers. This prayer is performed every night during Ramadan. People may use traditional Ramadan greetings such as "Ramadan Mubarak," which means "Blessed Ramadan," or "Ramadan Kareem," meaning "Generous Ramadan."

Many Muslims see Ramadan as a month of reflection, community, and generosity. It is a time when Allah's mercy is believed to be most powerful. Fasting during Ramadan helps Muslims focus on Allah and exercise self-control. Muslims also believe that fasting makes them more aware of the hunger of people who are less fortunate. In some countries, many businesses schedule their hours around the Ramadan fast.

Many Muslims perform zakat, or acts of charity, during Ramadan. At the end of the month, many Muslims perform a special kind of zakat called Zakat al-Fitr. This is a gift of money to people who are less fortunate, so they can enjoy the feast of Eid al-Fitr. Originally, Muhammad decided the amount of food that people should donate during Ramadan. Today, most

GENEROSITY DURING RAMADAN

During Ramadan, Muslims donate millions of dollars to charity. It is considered the holiest time to perform good deeds or give zakat. Muslims also focus on helping others by volunteering, assisting relatives, and advocating for those in need. In New York, the charity Muslims Giving Back runs a food truck that feeds homeless people every day during Ramadan. Many mosques also provide free iftar meals for the community.

people give cash donations to charities that provide food for those in need.

Zakat is one of the five pillars of Islam, so it is required of every Muslim. During Ramadan, people are encouraged to pay zakat if they have enough money or savings to do so. In some countries, such as Saudi Arabia, zakat donations are collected by the government.

EID AL-FITR

Eid al-Fitr marks the end of Ramadan. A new crescent moon rises to mark the beginning of Shawwal, the month following Ramadan. Eid al-Fitr is celebrated during the first three days of Shawwal. In Muslim-populated countries, it is a national holiday. On Eid al-Fitr, the month of fasting comes to an end.

Eid al-Fitr is a huge social occasion that involves feasting and gift giving. Since Muslims live in different places around the world, many Eid traditions are connected with local

PERSPECTIVES

A RAMADAN RUN FOR CHARITY

Many Muslims work hard to be generous during Ramadan. In England, Haroon Mota ran 161.5 miles (260 km) while fasting during Ramadan in 2020. He ran 6.2 miles (10 km) each evening at 8:00 p.m. before breaking his daily fast. In total, Mota raised more than $68,000 for a Muslim charity. Haroon said, "It was such hard work staying motivated to run daily for 30 days whilst feeling thirsty, hungry, experiencing dehydration and fatigue, but it's been such a successful fundraiser that it makes every bit of the struggle worthwhile. I ran voluntarily, but refugees are fleeing war and extreme poverty every day, and I ran for them."

and national cultures. For example, many women in South Asian countries get henna tattoos on their hands during Eid. Henna is a reddish-brown dye made from the powdered leaves of a plant native to North Africa and South Asia. The dye is used to color hair and create temporary skin tattoos. Henna body art is often applied during festive occasions.

On the first day of Eid, Muslims gather at mosques in the morning. Together, they join in communal prayer. Then the feast begins. Children receive presents such as new clothes, candy, and money. On this day, families may also visit the graves of relatives to pray for those who have passed away. Young people may visit the elderly, too. Special foods and sweets fill the tables.

Eid al-Fitr is a time of excitement for Muslims all over the world. It is a time for people to be with their families. People go to mosques and join in the Eid

In several countries, women and girls often get henna tattoos for special occasions such as weddings or Eid celebrations. Henna tattoos may feature floral patterns, intricate swirl designs, or Eid-themed symbols such as moons.

On Eid al-Fitr, crowds of people gather for prayers at mosques such as the Jama Masjid mosque in Delhi, India.

prayer with their communities. Afterward, people look back on the month of Ramadan and think about how they've become better people during that time. They think about their spiritual growth and give thanks as they celebrate with family and friends.

STRAIGHT TO THE SOURCE

In some places, Muslims face religious discrimination. In the United States, everyone has the right to practice his or her own religion. At the beginning of Ramadan in 2023, President Joe Biden made a statement recognizing Muslim Americans:

> *During this holy month, we . . . honor Muslim communities across our nation. . . . From science and technology, to arts and academia, to law and medicine, to business and government, and beyond—Muslim Americans continue to strengthen our nation's diverse tapestry generation after generation. So today, let us join together across cultures and faiths and renew our commitment to creating a more equal, more just, more tolerant, and more compassionate nation. To my fellow Americans observing Ramadan, and to Muslims around the world: Ramadan Kareem.*

Source: "Statement from President Joe Biden on the Occasion of Ramadan." *White House*, 22 Mar. 2023, whitehouse.gov. Accessed 18 Jun. 2023.

WHAT'S THE BIG IDEA?

Take a close look at this passage. What is the main purpose of Biden's statement? What can you tell about the various roles Muslim Americans have played in US society?

IMPORTANT DATES

Approximately 570 CE
The prophet Muhammad is born in Mecca.

610
The angel Jibreel appears to Muhammad and begins to reveal the Qur'an. Muhammad begins receiving revelations from Allah.

613
Muhammad begins sharing the revelations he receives with people in Mecca.

622
Muhammad and his followers flee to Medina.

624
Muhammad receives a revelation commanding Muslims to fast for 30 days.

630
Muslims return to Mecca.

Approximately 650
The first written copy of the Qur'an is completed.

1500s–1800s
Nearly 40,000 Muslims are brought to the Americas and enslaved.

1915
The first official mosque is built in New York City.

1985
The first Arab and first Muslim astronaut, Sultan Al Saud, observes Ramadan aboard the space shuttle Discovery.

STOP AND THINK

Dig Deeper

After reading this book, what questions do you still have about Ramadan and Eid al-Fitr? With an adult's help, find a few reliable sources that can help you answer your questions. Write a paragraph about what you learned.

Say What?

Studying holidays and cultural history can mean learning a lot of new vocabulary. Find five words in this book you've never heard before. Use a dictionary to find out what they mean. Then write the meanings in your own words and use each word in a new sentence.

You Are There

This book discusses Eid al-Fitr celebrations. Imagine you are attending an Eid al-Fitr celebration in your neighborhood. Write a journal entry describing your experience. What decorations do you see? What type of activities do you participate in? Be sure to add plenty of detail to your notes.

Another View

This book talks about Ramadan celebrations around the world. As you know, every source is different. Ask a librarian or another adult to help you find another source about Ramadan traditions. Write a short essay comparing and contrasting the new source's point of view with that of this book's author. What is the point of view of each author? How are they similar and why? How are they different and why?

GLOSSARY

convert
to change to a different religion

fast
to avoid eating and drinking

immigrate
to move to and resettle in a new country

mosque
a building used for worship by Muslims

prophet
a person who receives and relays a message believed to be from God

prostrate
to stretch out with one's face and hands on the ground in submission to God

revelation
a message from God

solemn
with seriousness and dignity

sultan
a Muslim king or ruler

ONLINE RESOURCES

To learn more about Ramadan and Eid al-Fitr, visit our free resource websites below.

Core Library CONNECTION
FREE! COMMON CORE MULTIMEDIA RESOURCES

Visit **abdocorelibrary.com** or scan this QR code for free Common Core resources for teachers and students, including vetted activities, multimedia, and booklinks, for deeper subject comprehension.

Booklinks NONFICTION NETWORK
FREE! ONLINE NONFICTION RESOURCES

Visit **abdobooklinks.com** or scan this QR code for free additional online weblinks for further learning. These links are routinely monitored and updated to provide the most current information available.

LEARN MORE

Ali, S. K., and Aisha Saeed. *Once upon an Eid.* Amulet Books, 2020.

Kehoe, Rachel. *A Look at Islam*. BrightPoint, 2023.

Shaffi, Sarah. *All about Eid: Things to Make and Do*. Scholastic, 2021.

INDEX

About the Author

Bev Crawford is an author who writes both fiction and nonfiction for kids and adults. She loves to try new foods from around the world. She is curious about most things, loves research, and especially enjoys hiking with her dog in the woods around Connecticut.